The 4 Components of Powerful You! PRIMARY

Social Skills St

Each A-Z **Powerful You** lesson includes a story of a child that you already know from your experiences of working with children. The children's names may be different, but the stories are similar. As you share these stories with your current students, remind them that these are about YOUR former students. Sharing these stories with a confidence that you are talking about students you know, allows the A-Z **Powerful You** kids to come alive.

Positive Self-talk

Positive self-talk is anything you might quietly say in your head to help you cope with a stressful situation or to calm down. Instead of allowing negative thoughts to take over, teach children to train their brain in a positive way. Children will memorize and say each phrase in their head during a difficult time. By the end of the year, they will recite the full A-Z **Powerful You** self-talk and use it in their daily life.

Practice/Role-play

Engaging students in drama and movement motivates the child to participate and enhances recall. Role-playing school situations (while holding the **Powerful You** Educator Card) will help the student store information in both the body and the brain.

Draw/Write

Each lesson shows a thinking map that will help students organize their thoughts in a way that's easy to understand. The following thinking maps are used: Circle map to define and brainstorm, bubble map to describe, tree map to classify or sort, brace map to identify the parts of a whole, flow map to sequence, and the multi-flow map to understand cause/effect.

  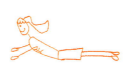 

The Magical Calming Tool

Deep breathing is widely accepted as one of the most effective tools to teach kids to calm down. We must practice this skill during calm moments rather than meltdown moments. Practice deep breathing BEFORE each **Powerful You** lesson.

But watch out, you might feel the benefits, too!

- Sit on your chair with your feet flat on the ground or sit cross legged on the floor.
- Press your bottom into your chair (ground) as you stretch your spine tall.
- Breathe in through your nose while stretching your arms above your head.
- Breathe out through your nose while lowering your arms to your side.
- INHALE deeper to the count of 4. EXHALE slower and longer to the count of 8.
- Continue filling your LUNGS with fresh oxygen for 5-10 breaths. Practice daily.

Social Skills Lessons

A	Attentive Al - Listening
B	Brave Betsy - Separation Anxiety
C	Controlled Cal - Self-Control
D	Different Diane - Family Diversity
E	Energetic Erica - Healthy Behaviors
F	Forgiving Floyd - Apologizing
G	Good Sport Grady - Teamwork
H	Honest Holden - Honesty
I	Ignoring Ina - Ignoring Distractions
J	Joking Jodi - Appropriate Play
K	Kind Kelly - Kindness
L	Loving Logan - Resilience
M	Mindful Maria - Managing Emotions
N	No-fear Nate - Worry
O	Okay Odie - Accepting Change
P	Problem Solving Pat - Independent Problem Solving
Q	Questioning Quinton - Thinking Before Questioning
R	Responsible Reese - Responsibility
S	Stick with it Stan - Grit
T	Turn-taker Trish - Sharing
U	Uplifting Uma - Giving Compliments
V	Voicing Viv - Standing Up for Yourself
W	Waiting to Speak Willa - Waiting To Speak
X	Xpressing Xander - Expressing Feelings
Y	Yes Ma'am Yuri - Obeying Safety Rules
Z	Zesty Zhen - Goal Setting

Powerful you!
PRIMARY

Powerful You
Positive Self-talk

A	I am attentive.
B	I am brave.
C	I am in control.
D	I am unique.
E	I am full of energy.
F	I am forgiving.
G	I am a good sport.
H	I am honest.
I	I ignore distractions.
J	Joking has a time and place.
K	I have KIND hands, KIND feet, and KIND words.
L	I love myself.
M	I am calm.
N	I am the boss of my fears.
O	I am okay with change.
P	I am an independent problem solver.
Q	I ask "wh" questions.
R	I am responsible.
S	I stick with it.
T	I take turns.
U	I am an uplifter.
V	I use a strong voice.
W	I can wait.
X	I EXpress my feelings.
Y	I say YES to rules.
Z	I practice with zest.

Powerful You! PRIMARY

A ATTENTIVE AL

POSITIVE SELF-TALK

"I am attentive."

{ Listen }

When Al went to kindergarten, he did not know how to listen. He rolled on the floor, shouted out in class, and interrupted his teacher when she was talking. The teacher said, "Al, pay attention!" Everyone was happy the day he learned these five listening tips (repeat after me):

- I keep my eyes on the teacher (point to eyes).
- I keep my body still (hug yourself).
- I have listening ears (point to both ears - You can't listen and talk at the same time).
- I raise my hand when I have a question (raise one hand).
- I never give up (pump your fist)!

Now Al listens to the teacher the first time.

→ Practice ←

Listen to your teacher using the above listening tips as he/she calls these movements: tiptoe to your desk, pat your head and rub your belly, hop on one foot, touch alternating knees as you march, spin your body two times, and sit down.

Draw/Write

Al used his whole body to pay attention. Write or draw how you use all your body parts to listen.

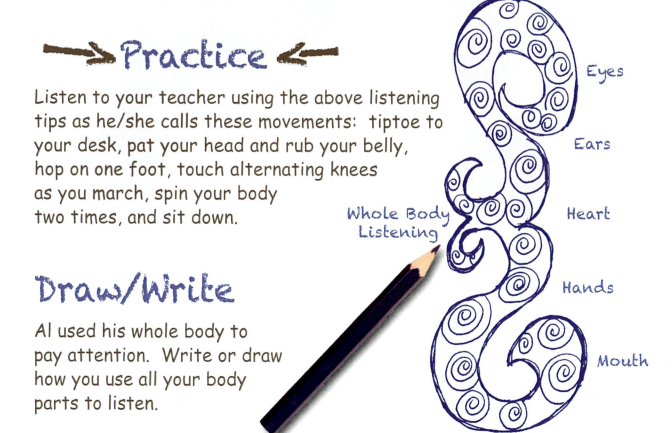

Whole Body Listening — Eyes, Ears, Heart, Hands, Mouth

{ Listen }

Betsy cried every morning when she went to school. Her stomach hurt and her hands felt sweaty saying goodbye to her mom. Then Betsy learned the five second goodbye. She hugged her mom and said, "I LOVE YOU." Then, she turned and walked away without looking back. Betsy said in her head, "I am brave." Doing this quickly helped them both say goodbye. Betsy felt proud when she walked into class on her own. Shhh- Don't tell anybody, but she still carried her mom's picture in her pocket!

→Practice←

Being independent means doing things on your own with little help from your parents. Act out things you do independently in the morning to get ready for school. Let your friends guess what you are doing.

Write

Betsy got ready every morning by following a morning list.
Draw or write your "get ready for school" routine.

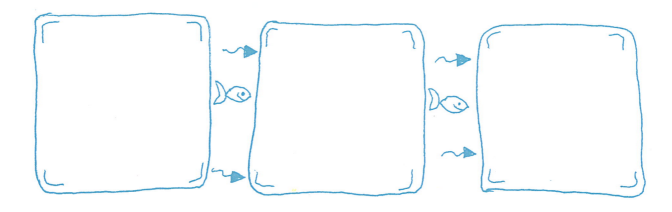

C CONTROLLED Cal

POSITIVE SELF-TALK
"I am in control."

{ Listen }

A classmate took Cal's ball away at recess. Cal felt hot, his heart raced, and his face scrunched up. His body screamed, "I AM ANGRY!" To be in control, Cal did the following:

- Hands went into his pockets so they didn't hurt others.
- Tongue went to the roof of his mouth so mean words did not come out.
- Legs walked away and body breathed deeply to calm down.
- Thoughts changed to: "I am in control."

Cal felt happy when he used self-control to calm down.

→ Practice ←

Your friend breaks your favorite toy, and you want to hit him. Act out what you do to stay in control with your hands, your tongue, your legs and body, and your thoughts.

Draw/Write

Cal used self-control when someone took his ball away. Draw or write things that make you angry.

I feel angry when

DIFFERENT Diane

POSITIVE SELF-TALK
"I am unique."

{ Listen }

Diane felt like she was the only one in her school whose dad did not come to the Donuts for Dad's celebration. She felt sad that he was never around. She brought her uncle instead and sat next to someone else who brought their grandpa. She noticed all families may look different on the outside, but on the inside, a family gives love and kindness. Later, her uncle took her for ice cream and to the park. She felt loved.

→ Practice ←

Without using words, act out ways your family gives you love. Let your friends guess what you are doing.

Draw/Write

Diane's family showed love by taking her for ice cream and to the park. Write or draw ways your family shows love (don't forget your pets).

My family shows love by

E ENERGETIC Erica

POSITIVE SELF-TALK

"I am full of energy."

{ Listen }

Erica loved moving. When she got up in the morning, she ate a healthy breakfast and practiced breathing and stretching. During school she moved quietly like a cat so she wouldn't disturb others. Wiggling her toes and twiddling her thumbs under her desk helped her sit still when the teacher talked. When school was out, she played outside until the sun went down. Erica went to bed early so she was well rested.

→ Practice ←

One person in your class pretends to be Energetic Erica. Everyone closes their eyes as Erica moves around the room so no one hears her. Erica changes one thing in the room. Open your eyes and guess what changed in the room.

Draw/Write

Erica enjoyed being active. Draw or write things you do for a healthy body.

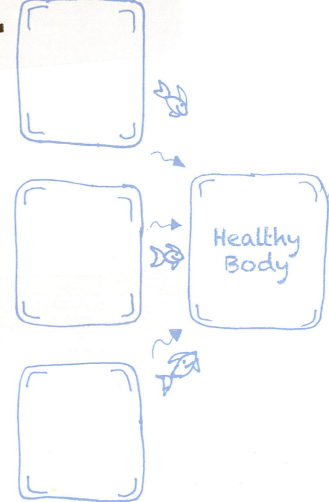

F FORGIVING Floyd

POSITIVE SELF-TALK
"I am forgiving."

{ Listen }

Floyd was playing tag when another student ran into him. The student looked at Floyd and quickly said, "I am sorry. It was an accident." Apologizing quickly allowed the boys to talk and understand each other. Floyd said, "I forgive you." They learned from this accident to be aware of personal space.

→ Practice ←

One person accidentally runs into another. Quickly apologize by saying "I am sorry. It was an accident." The other student says, "I forgive you."

Draw/Write

Write a letter of apology or draw a picture of someone you have hurt. Write: I am sorry I _____ (say what you did that was hurtful).

Next time I will_____
(tell what you will do so no one is hurt).

I am sorry I _____
_____
_____
_____

Next time I will
_____
_____
_____
_____
_____
_____

G GOOD SPORT Grady

POSITIVE SELF-TALK

"I am a good sport"

{ Listen }

Good Sport Grady believed that everyone in his class was important and good at something! WORKING TOGETHER WAS FUN! During clean-up time, Grady was the first to put the blocks in the basket and then help others. At lunch, he encouraged everyone to work together to clean up the table so they would earn a bright star. When the kids had trouble jumping rope, you'd hear Grady say, "KEEP TRYING! YOU CAN DO IT! DON'T GIVE UP!" Everyone was a winner in Grady's class when they pitched in with kindness and tried their best!

→ Practice ←

PLAY THE BUSY BEE GAME.
- All students stand back to back with a partner.
- If there is an odd number, the teacher can play.
- When the teacher shouts out, "Busy Bees," students must switch partners in 3 seconds without talking.
- The teacher will continue saying, "Busy Bees" until all kids have partnered with everyone in class. Everyone's a winner!

Write

Being a good sport by working together as a team was important to Grady. Write about how you can be a team player in your classroom.

Teamwork

HONEST Holden

POSITIVE SELF-TALK
"I am honest."

{ Listen }

Holden did not have money to buy a new pencil. He wanted Sam's sparkly one, so he snatched it from his desk when no one was looking. When the teacher asked who took Sam's pencil, Holden felt scared and said, "Not me." That night Holden was worried and said, "I took the pencil!" He felt better when he was honest. He returned the pencil to Sam and said, "I am sorry." From that day forward, Holden took only what was his and told the truth.

→ Practice ←

Play the "MY FAVORITE" game. A student says a sentence about themselves such as, "My favorite vegetable is carrots." The class chooses if the sentence is true (honest) or not true.

Draw/Write

Holden felt worried when he was dishonest. Draw or write what can happen when you are dishonest.

Dishonesty

I IGNORING Ina

POSITIVE SELF-TALK

"I ignore distractions."

{ Listen }

Ina liked the classroom to be quiet so she could get her work finished. But sometimes the kids at her table distracted her by talking and playing during work time. When this happened, Ina turned her back away from them and kept her eyes on her work. Ignoring distractions allowed her to get her work done so she could have center time.

→ Practice ←

Sit at your desk and keep your eyes focused on your paper. One student will be assigned as the distracting student by tapping your shoulder or making loud sounds. Turn your back away and keep looking at your paper. Take turns being the distracting student.

Draw/Write

Talking and playing in class distracted Ina and caused her to not get work finished. Draw or write about things that distract you.

I get distracted when

J JOKING Jodi

POSITIVE SELF-TALK
"Joking has a time & place."

{ Listen }

Jodi was the new student and wanted the other kids to like her. She made silly faces and loud inappropriate noises to get the kids to laugh. She thought if she joked with the other kids during class, they would want to be her friend. But, her silliness got her in trouble during learning time! Being silly has a time and place! Now, Jodi is silly during recess and at home, but never when the teacher is talking.

→ Practice ←

Pretend you are the new kid and want a friend. Practice the following with a classmate.

- Use eye contact, smile and ask a classmate to play with you at recess.
- Smile and say hello to someone new. Invite them to sit with you at lunch.
- Look friendly and ask someone a question such as, "What games do you like to play?"

Write

Jodi loves to have fun.

Describe qualities you like in a friend.

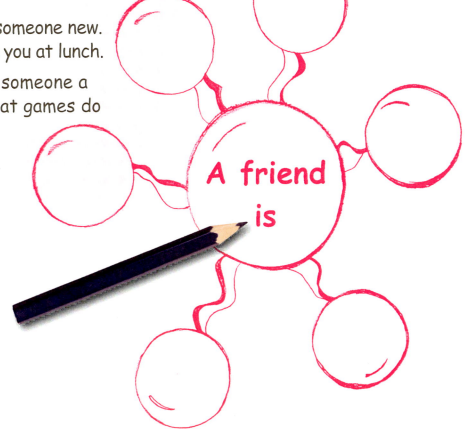

POSITIVE SELF-TALK

"I have KIND hands, KIND feet, and KIND words."

{ Listen }

Kelly showed up for school everyday with kind hands, kind feet, and kind words. She used her kind hands to help others tie their shoes, push in chairs, and clean up the classroom. She kept her feet to herself and stayed a hula hoop space from others. She used kind words like please and thank you to show respect to adults. Kind Kelly was proud to receive the outstanding citizen award in her school.

⟶ Practice ⟵

Role-play the following situations by adding kindness:
- A new student comes into your class crying and holding his mom's leg.
- Your classroom is a mess and it is time to go home.
- While your class is playing at recess, one student is sitting alone.

Draw/Write

Kelly never uses her hands to hurt others. Write or draw things you do with your hands to be helpful and kind.

L LOVING Logan

POSITIVE SELF-TALK
"I love myself."

{ Listen }

One student laughed at Logan and called him "orange top" because of his bright orange hair. Instead of feeling sad, Logan brushed those words off his shoulders and refused to take them inside his body. He laughed in his head and said, "I love myself the way I am." He was grateful for his healthy body, smart brain, kind heart, and HIS UNIQUE HAIR!

→ Practice ←

The sign for "I love you" in American Sign Language is the pinky finger, index finger, and thumb pointed straight (with the middle two fingers held down in the palm). Learn this language and point it towards yourself to be reminded that you are loved.

Draw/Write

Logan loved himself. Draw or write things you love about yourself.

Things I love about myself

MINDFUL Maria

POSITIVE SELF-TALK
"I am calm."

{ Listen }

Maria's body told her when she was frustrated. Her heart beat fast, her skin got hot, and tears came out her eyes. This usually happened when she didn't get her way. She learned to go to the Calm Down Corner in her classroom BEFORE the feeling became too strong. In the Calm Down Corner, she pressed a squishy ball, breathed 5-10 deep breaths, and said in her head, "I am calm." Listening to her body helped Maria calm down BEFORE she exploded.

→ Practice ←

Calming down BEFORE your feelings get too big helps you be in control. Play the Before Game. The teacher will say the following sentences as you play.
- Hop on one foot 5 times BEFORE you squat down low.
- Do 7 jumping jacks BEFORE you touch your toes 3 times.
- Take 5 deep breaths BEFORE you punch your fist in your hand.

Draw/Write

Everyone gets frustrated and needs a place to calm down. Write or draw about what you do to calm down when your feelings are BIG AND STRONG.

I calm down by

NO-FEAR Nate

POSITIVE SELF-TALK

"I am the BOSS of my fears."

{ Listen }

Nate hated going to bed at night because he felt afraid. His body felt tense and his breath quickened. To combat FEAR, Nathan made a sleep plan. First, he said in his head, "I am the boss of my fears." Next, he looked under his bed and around his room. He asked his mom to check on him until he fell asleep. Then, he breathed deeply and hugged his stuffed animal, which he always took to bed at night. Finally, Nate was able to be the boss of his fear and go to sleep.

→ Practice ←

- You are afraid to speak in your class because you feel others' eyes on you. Act out what you can do.
- You are afraid to spend the night at someone's house, but want to play with a friend. Act out what you can do.

Draw/Write

Nate was afraid at night. What makes you afraid or worried? Draw or write about your plan to be the boss of that fear!

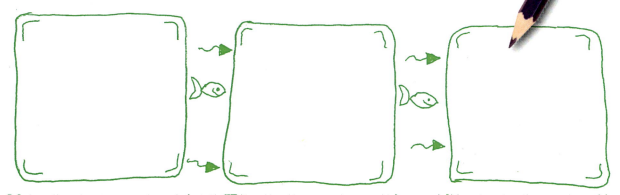

OKAY Odie

POSITIVE SELF-TALK

"I am okay with change."

{ Listen }

Odie's best friend, John, told him he was moving to another state. The class celebrated with chocolate cake and goodbye letters. At home he told his parents, "I am sad that John won't be at school anymore." They made plans to write and visit him in his new town. The next morning, the teacher let Odie sit at John's desk. Odie said quietly in his head, "I am okay with change."

→ Practice ←

Change might cause sadness. Pretend a classmate is sad. Act out what you can say or do to brighten their day.

Draw/Write

Odie felt sad when his friend moved away. Draw or write about what makes you sad.

I feel sad when

P PROBLEM SOLVING ▸ Pat

POSITIVE SELF-TALK
"I am a problem solver."

{ Listen }

Pat was a problem solver. Pat used I.P.S. - Independent Problem Solving. Before asking his teacher for help, he tried to figure things out on his own. Instead of crying when he had a problem, he followed the "3 Before Me" rule. He thought of 3 different solutions and tried them before asking for help from his teacher. Here are just a few things he tried: Sharing, trading, taking turns, using words, deep breathing, ignoring, getting help from a friend, talking to parents, walking away, or using rock-paper-scissors.

⟶ Practice ⟵

Use the "3 Before Me" rule and solve these problems on your own:
- Your crayon broke. What can you do?
- You can't tie your shoes.
- Someone cut you in line.

Draw/Write

Pat thought of solutions to problems. Write or draw 3 things you can do if you want the same ball or toy that someone is playing with at recess.

When I want the same thing as a friend, I can

Q QUESTIONING Quinton

POSITIVE SELF-TALK
"I ask "wh" questions."

{ Listen }

Quinton knew that his brain needed time to think before asking a question. When raising his hand, he made sure his questions were used to learn something new or to better understand something. Most of Quinton's questions began with the wh sound, like in the words: what, where, when, or why.

→ Practice ←

Sit in a classroom circle with your teacher in the center. Using the question word "what", ask your teacher questions that find out what he/she likes, dislikes, wishes, and is good at. Your teacher will reply in a complete sentence.

Draw/Write

After asking your teacher "what" questions, draw or write about your teacher.

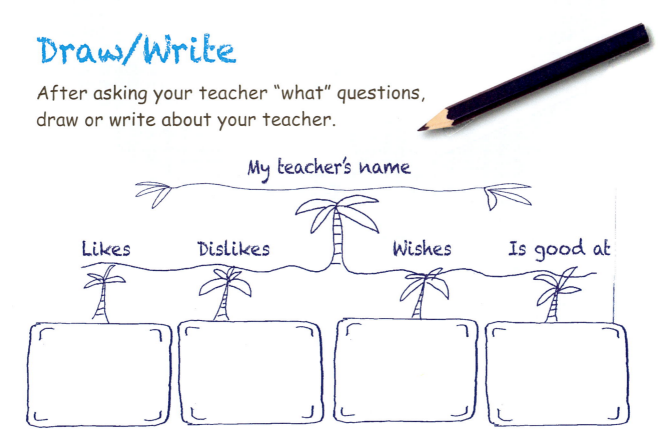

My teacher's name

Likes Dislikes Wishes Is good at

Responsible Reese

R RESPONSIBLE Reese

POSITIVE SELF-TALK

"I am responsible."

{ Listen }

Reese left for school with her shirt on backwards and her shoes untied. At school, Reese's pencil holder was a disaster and she could NEVER find her homework! One day her teacher saw her put her homework paper in the proper file. She said, "Reese, you are being so responsible! I bet that feels good inside your body!!" It did feel good. REESE FELT PROUD! Reese smiled big and thought in her head, "I am responsible!" From that moment forward, Reese made a shift to stay organized and turn in her work on time. She even earned the Neat Desk Award!

→ Practice ←

Play the Responsible Bear Game. Bears must move responsibly without pushing others. The teacher will scatter 8 hula hoops about on the floor. When the music plays, you will be a "bear" quietly wandering about looking for a "cave" to hide in. You may hop, skip or dance while music plays. When the music stops, you must step into a "cave" (hoop) and make your best "bear growl." After you have completed this, the teacher will take away 2 of the hoops and repeat the activity until there are only 3 hoops left. Practice moving without touching others.

Draw/Write

You are responsible for what you say and do. How do you show responsibility in your class?

I am responsible when I

S › STICK WITH IT › Stan

POSITIVE SELF-TALK
"I stick with it."

{ Listen }

Stan joined martial arts for the first time. On the 2nd week he told his mom that he didn't want to go. His mom said to him, "If you stay home, you will not get to play on your ipad for the rest of the week." Stan put on his uniform, proudly tied his belt and ate a healthy snack. He said in his head, "I stick with it." Stan gave 100% effort at his lesson and earned a red stripe by showing confidence and eye contact. He thanked his mom for teaching him to not give up on something new!

→ Practice ←

Act out something new you would like to try. Let your friends guess what they think you are doing.

Think/Write

Stan planned his after school routine.
Draw or write about your after school routine.

T TURN-TAKER Trish

POSITIVE SELF-TALK
"I take turns."

{ Listen }

Every day Trish raced her friends to the playground to grab a swing. She told others, "I go first!" Others stopped playing with her because she did not take turns. When friends came to her house, she bossed them around and would not share her toys. One day she said, "YOU go first." It felt good to watch others have fun. Once she learned how to share, the other children wanted to play with her.

→ Practice ←

Act out two people wanting the same ball. Practice saying the following:
"Today, you go first. Can we trade in five minutes? Do you want to play together?"

Draw/Write

Trish learned that when you are bossy, others don't want to play with you. Draw or write what can happen when you are a bossy friend.

U
Uplifting Uma

U UPLIFTING Uma

POSITIVE SELF-TALK

"I am an uplifter."

{ Listen }

Uma's class was grumpy right before spring break. They complained when they didn't get their favorite snack and argued over carrying the lunch basket. Kids tattled on their friends for just about everything. Not Uplifting Uma! She smiled at others and used kind words such as, "I like your neat work." Instead of tattling, she found the good in her classmates and complimented them.

→ Practice ←

One classmate stands in the center. The class takes turns complimenting that friend. Use kind words to make them smile.

Write/Draw

Uma said kind things to her classmates. Write or draw what happens in your class when you tattle and argue.

VOICING Viv

POSITIVE SELF-TALK

"I use a strong voice."

{ Listen }

Viv always loved school. But one day when the teacher wasn't looking, a classmate pinched her and said she didn't want to be Viv's friend. Viv felt scared so she talked to her parents that night. Her parents said, "Viv, use your strong voice and tell her to stop!" The next day, Viv stood tall and said, "Stop pinching me." Then she added, "If you don't stop, I will REPORT you." The pinching stopped.

→Practice←

Someone is calling you names. Use your strong voice and tell them to STOP. Tell them you will REPORT them if they do not stop.

Draw/Write

A REPORT is used to tell an adult about danger. Name and draw pictures of the adults in your school or community who will listen to your report of repeated unkindness, threats, or danger.

Adults who help me stay safe

W WAITING TO SPEAK Willa

POSITIVE SELF-TALK
"I can wait."

{ Listen }

Waiting to speak was hard for Willa. She talked but never listened. She learned that TALKING WAS LIKE PLAYING CATCH! One person talked and the other person listened. The conversation went back and forth just like throwing and catching a ball. Now, Willa is a better friend because she listens while her friends are talking.

→ Practice ←

Buddy up with a partner and a crayon. The crayon will be called the "talking stick." The partner holding the "talking stick" will talk, while the other partner quietly listens and keeps eye contact. Partners pass the "talking stick" back and forth while communicating. The teacher will give the following cue to open the conversation: "Talk to your partner about your family."

Draw/Write

Waiting to talk was hard for Willa. Draw or write about when it is hard for you to wait.

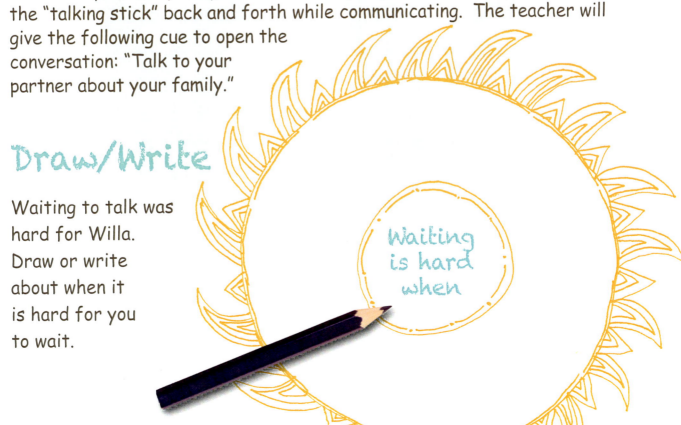

Waiting is hard when

X XPRESSING Xander

POSITIVE SELF-TALK
"I express my feelings."

{ Listen }

Xander thought when he whined and complained, his teacher would give him what he wanted. Sometimes he cried, yelled and threw things when he was angry or sad. His teacher said, "Xander, use your words." Xander noticed his frustrations passed quickly when he told how he felt. Now, when his feelings are STRONG, Xander takes a deep breath and calmly says how he feels.

→ Practice ←

Telling an adult how you feel can make you feel better. Practice expressing yourself when you are afraid, excited, disappointed, happy, sad, and proud. Say, "I feel___ when_____."

Draw/Write

Xander can look at a friend's face and tell how they feel. Draw faces and write about your feelings.

Feelings

Happy   Sad   Mad   Scared

y "YES, MA'AM" Yuri

POSITIVE SELF-TALK

"I say YES to school rules."

{ Listen }

Yuri was shocked when he came to school for the first time and had to follow rules. He wanted to run in the halls, balance on top of the monkey bars, and swing on his belly. He did not understand that rules at school keep everyone safe and orderly for learning. One day he chose to run up the slide, even though he was told to use the steps. Yuri fell backwards and broke his arm! From that day forward he followed the school rules.

→ Practice ←

Go on a safety field trip at your school. Look for crosswalk signs, poison labels, fire drill instructions, wet floor signs, and playground signs. Find soap, tissues, and trash cans that prevent germs from spreading.

Write/Draw

Yuri hurt himself because he didn't follow school rules. What can happen when you don't obey school rules?

Z ZESTY Zhen

POSITIVE SELF-TALK
"I practice with zest."

{ Listen }

Zhen dreamed of making it across the monkey bars. Everyday she practiced with ZEST (energy) until one day she went all the way across. She felt proud by never giving up on her goal! She did the same with her schoolwork. When Zhen did not know how to count to 20, she practiced at home until she learned. She never gave up! Practicing with ZEST helped her reach her goal.

→ Practice ←

Play Push Up Math. Get in push up position (you can use your knees). Touch alternating shoulders each time and count to 20. Can you count by 2's in push up position?

Draw/Write

Zhen's goal was to go across the monkey bars and get better at math. Draw or write things you will practice to reach your goals.

Things I will practice